My Throat Is Full of Songbirds

Love
& Blessings
martina

My Throat Is Full of Songbirds

Martina Nicholson, MD

Old Mountain Press

Published by:
Old Mountain Press, Inc.
2542 S. Edgewater Dr.
Fayetteville, NC 28303

www.oldmountainpress.com

Copyright © 2005 Martina Nicholson, MD
Interior text design by Tom Davis
ISBN: 1-931575-60-6
Library of Congress Control Number: 2005934464

My Throat Is Full of Songbirds
All rights reserved. Except for brief excerpts used in reviews, no portion of this work may be reproduced or published without expressed written permission from the author or the author's agent.

First Edition
Printed and bound in the United States of America by Morris Publishing • www.morrispublishing.com • 800-650-7888
1 2 3 4 5 6 7 8 9 10

For my colleagues and patients as well as my family and friends. The mysteries of the life we share in our various roles have inspired these poems. Thanks to each of you for your gifts to me. May you be richly blessed.

CONTENTS

CINDERELLA'S SLIPPER 9
SNOW WHITE 10
AVE AND JIM AT THE PIANO 11
BROKEN WING 12
CANTICLE WITH A NEW VOICE 13
COME HOME NOW, JOE 14
DIFFERENT WAYS TO PRAY 15
DUET 16
FIDELITY (Simone and Sartre) 17
FIESTA FOR THE CAMARILLOS 18
GLORY LAND 20
GOD LOVES US LIKE A MOTHER 21
AVALANCHED HEART 22
THE MARTYR OF EL MOZOTE 23
BEAUTY 24
BEING JUST PILGRIMS 25
BREATHING LESSONS 26
FAITH 27
MARRIAGE, TOO, HAS SEASONS 28
I COULD HAVE BEEN A LADY 30
IGUAZU FALLS 31
"I LET HER GO GENTLY" 33
IN THE GRAVEYARD 34
PATTYCAKE 35
MI AMOR, MI COMPAÑERO DEL CAMINO 36
MOONBEAMS IN A JAR 37
WRESTLING WITH THE ANGEL 38
MRI SCAN 39
MY SON 40
MY MAILBOX 41
ON THE BENCH IN FRONT OF THE CLINIC .. 42
PRAYER FOR THE BLUEBIRD 44
PRAYING WITH BOTH HANDS 45

RAIN GOD	46
RUMPELSTILTSKIN'S MAID	47
THE GEESE	48
THE REAL RAPUNZEL	49
WATCHING YOU PLAY THE PIANO	50
WHITE MOTHS IN MOONLIGHT	52
LIVE THE QUESTIONS	53
SANDWICHES	54
THE HOSE WITH THE KINK	55
THE GUARDIAN ANGEL OF THE RED BUS	56
ÉLAN VITAL	58
DANCING WITH THE MINISTER OF THE INTERIOR	59
ALBONDIGA SOUP	60
CANNING TOMATOES	61
ISABEL	62
PICNIC AT THE CHUMASH BURIAL GROUND, 1963	64
PLAY THE SAXOPHONE FOR ME, JAMIE	66
THIS JAR OF JAM	67
HOLY GROUND	lxviii

CINDERELLA'S SLIPPER

It is made of glass,
And holds light like a prism,
It's for a tiny foot,
Magical as Thumbelina's,
Or Tinkerbell's.

Way past midnight,
Pumpkins and mice,
Rags and ashes,
The glass slipper
Stays in the prince's grasp.

The miracle that made it
Lost the rest;
Lost for her the briefest grace,
The gown and the ballroom,
The dance like dreaming.

In the morning at the cold hearth,
Scrubbing floors,
Snubbed by stepsisters,
And wicked stepmother;
Doing the daily heap of tasks,
Playing with mice and spiders.

Under her mattress is the other one,
The ethereal glass,
Holding moonbeams in the night,
When she takes it out to remember.

SNOW WHITE

The witch looked in the mirror.
Not enough,
Not enough.
Beautiful; but not enough.
Not the fairest in the land.

Snow white skin,
Rose red cheeks,
Ebony black hair.
And what can not be seen,
Her kindness and humility.

You and I can still see her perfectly.

And what if there were a photograph?
Even if she dies,
Even if the witch should kill her,
Even if she's underground,
The photo would tell the truth.

The photograph would be enough
To keep her safe;
You see there is no lying there.

And even if you tear it up,
You can remember her face,
And its insistent beauty.

AVE AND JIM AT THE PIANO

The melody pours out of the baby grand,
And Nana stands,
Lifting her arms out to the side,
As she has done since before I was born—
She is inviting us into the embrace of her song;
Dad plays, with his glasses down on his nose,
And his tongue lolling in his mouth,
And when he remembers, and knows the next chord,
He sings the harmony.

Nana's voice lifts off like seagulls in the sunset,
Rising with iridescent wings,
Her tremolo fills the house,
Her contralto like honey; like melted sunlight
On the ocean just before sunset;
A true path to heaven.

Oh, tender songs at twilight,
Songs written in the pre-war early 1900's,
When all the world was young and gay;
When it was possible to believe that mankind was perfectible
And cultured;
And that the world I was growing into would be a world
With so much leisure we would all sing, all the time;
Full of love and joy,
And heaven on earth.

Nana's songs, Dad's songs,
 The songs they played and sang together,
Songs to make your heart break on beauty,
Songs to melt you,
 And to deepen your soul,
Songs calling you to paradise.

BROKEN WING

When the mind is
Flying with a broken wing
You must believe that
The heart knows
The soul knows;
You must remember
With mindless remembering,
Where safety is,
Where the meadow and soft grasses lie.

Use the wind to ride the storm,
With the upper wing at a slightly tilted angle
To correct for the broken one,
And with the other birds very close,
Flying the updrafts to help you.

CANTICLE WITH A NEW VOICE

Heaven is endlessly possible:
Green chartreuse leaves on the arthritic old tree,
Red poppies on the road to the Cathedral;
Walk through any of these doors.
Music is the easiest path to the unknown;
Notes dancing up through shiny silence,
Somehow, new harmonies unguessed
Lead you through the hole in the wall:
Snow is another way to hide and find the cleanest path.

Because heaven is not time or space
We can all be there together,
Like animals who huddle together against the cold
Keeping what matters close to our chests;
Our hands cupping the little flame,
Bitter winter all around us.
We can follow the chartreuse leaves
Which have just appeared on the old apple tree,
Or dive into the scarlet poppies,
Their cheeks full of springtime;
Every path is new as one covered with a clean spring snow.

COME HOME NOW, JOE

Come home now, Joe,
Come home;
While spring is in the morning air,
And all the blooms are limned with light,
Come home and make me laugh.

Come now, while all the while
Your voice and charm
Can make the laughter fall like silver
From the spring in me;
All full from winter rains.

Come home; and while the hours
Are brimming gold and warm,
Like daffodils and valentines
Against the old stone walls,

Take me in your arms
And hold the sun against my bones.

We know it will be evening
Soon, as every day before;
So come home, now,
While there is time,
The door is open wide,
And there's sunlight on the floor.

DIFFERENT WAYS TO PRAY

I ask you what to do in this moment to make it right; to not
    mess it up?

I ask you what to do
to make the grace flow from you,
 like juice from the ripest oranges.

To make it flow onto someone who has a tongue so parched
and a life so like a desert;
someone who never knew oranges existed,
can't imagine their sweetness,
can't believe it is possible for the dry mouth
 to stop being that dry,
that thirsty;
for juice that sunrise color to flow down the throat
in a swallow made for an angel.

Oh, Lord,
Give me those heavenly oranges,
Give me that much juice.

DUET

My throat is full of songbirds;
a candle burning in my mind
through this dark night,
like jazz, the notes well up, full of groans,
pre-dawn moonlight and shadows.

Morning comes: hello in sunshine,
this is what I meant to say!
clear water falls from high ledges
I lift my face in that limpid stream
and sing the psalm-words.

they rise like clouds:
water hidden in such small droplets
we cannot see them in this misty substance.

You spend so much time listening;
like some medieval monk
deciphering a dusty score
in an illuminated manuscript;
bringing forth music
 Which looks just like blackbirds
Sitting on branches, curiously.
One wouldn't know they were singing.

FIDELITY (Simone and Sartre)

She would have given everything,
Her voice,
Her work,
Hollowed herself to a beautiful empty shell,
She would have been willing to stop thinking;
To be the only woman he made love with.
His true love,
His real partner,
His soul-mate.

But he twisted her love,
Called it all masters and slaves,
Got her to
Pimp fresh cunt for him:
He went ruthlessly on,
Saying that all that mattered
Is the "NOW"
And the personal freedom to choose;
To be able to do his solo pirouettes
Of the mind around any topic,
While fucking just anyone.

I am told that at the end of his life,
He realized he had been wrong;
He believed in God,
He believed in coherence
And divine mystery,
Even love;
He repented of his arrogance,
But no one read that last essay.
I don't know if she read it either.

FIESTA FOR THE CAMARILLOS

In August, in the morning
In Santa Barbara, on the beach
The white horses shimmer in the heat;
Their beautiful sexy butts--
Like white satin over dalmation freckles
In the pinker flesh where they join,
Like a crease in a valentine
Slither and shiver as they dance,
Flicking their long white tails aside
And prancing on silver-painted hoofs.

The silver saddles flash,
And women leaning low in red satin
Straddling the black leather and silver,
Breasts held tightly in red lace bolero jackets
 With the long flamenco sleeves,
White gloves holding reins of silver;
Jostle into line as we hear the band
Strike up the tune;

 And the horses,
Hearing those drums and that brass,
Nervous like teenagers at a dance,
Start tossing their white manes
Flicking their heads and snorting,
Arching their necks and lifting their feet
Just a little lighter off the ground
As we start toward State street;

Our thighs trying to hug
Through the satin the stiff leather
Of the parade saddles,
And we hold our heads proudly,
With the row of red carnations pinned at
The nape, making our heads heavy.

And when the townspeople
Lining the street cheer
"VIVA los Camarillos!"
We wave and smile,
And the horses prance.

GLORY LAND

I am yearning for you,
Glory land;
Where the tears we spill
God drinks in his cupped hands.

The blood He turns to wine,
Jesus' wine—the finest;
The bread is real,
 And warm from the oven.

Peace, flowing like a river,
Peace like liquid silver
Rolling over the waterfalls
And down the mountainsides,
Birds tangling themselves in the mists
Over the slabs of moving water.

Yes my Lord,
Peace,
Wine and bread,
Milk and honey,
Tears of joy.

GOD LOVES US LIKE A MOTHER

Oh, baby,
Oh, MY baby!
Oh funny-sweet-face-big-eyed toddler!
Oh tear-filled eyes!
Oh, my bunny-honey, sweet, big-bottom,
 Diaper-heavy fall-to-the-floor lamb-child!
Oh you, dancing in the sunlight to the big-boy music!
Skin incandescent and soft,
Naptime makes you heavy in my arms,
And I am glad to see the eyelashes on your cheeks,
The curl of your ears,
The way your hands cup over my breasts so protectively as you sleep!
Your momma loves you baby,
LOVES YOU, BABY!
Loves you even later when you slam the door,
And yell "NO"
Even when your face is smeared and bleared,
Even when you have pimples,
Even when you forget to come home.

Your momma loves you baby:
all the way to heartbreak
All the way back again;
Easy as the moon shining,
Easy as falling asleep, and waking up,
Easy as the days coming and going,
Watching you grow,
Big baby, honey, lamb-child, kiss-a-yo-face,
Breathing in and out,
My honey-lamb-child boy!

AVALANCHED HEART

I am a woman who
Lives in dreams,
Moves best in moonlight;
Seeks wisdom in the hidden things;
The way soap bubbles have that iridescence
Just before they burst.

I tried to become competent
To stop the bleeding and the dying
To bind up the wounds;
But it is everlasting
And no one is enough.

Dance and sing and cry;
There are not enough tears—
For a third of the world is dying of hunger.

Here, Lord,
Is my avalanched heart;
Under this mountain of pure snow.

THE MARTYR OF EL MOZOTE
(El Salvador, 1981)

They raped her over and over again,
But she kept singing.
They shot her,
And she kept singing.
They shot her again to stop her voice,
But still she sweetly sang.

Her broken body lying on the hill they called La Cruz,
Was just the cupful of her soul.

The sweet ethereal sound of her song
Kept floating into the soldiers' ears.
It drove them to fear and trembling,
Drove them almost to repentance,
Until someone took a machete
And cut off her head.

As the blood drained from her neck
They could still hear her song
In their undesiring ears.

Later, they remembered; and still heard,
And still trembled with their fear.

BEAUTY

Poor Bathsheba!

had she been fat,
with buck teeth,
or skimpy hair,
had sallow skin
or wilted breasts;
she might have been able
to sit on the roof after bathing,
while David's eyes dismissed her—
passing on to some other object of desire.

She could have gone down to dinner,
to her garden,
to her husband Uriah the Hittite
home dusty from war;
she could have had a child
who grew up in anonymity,
who loved her with devotion,
and who was not smitten
by the hand of the Lord
for the iniquities of his father.

She could have melted into the dusty rooftops
in the afternoon stillness and heat
as David's eyes wandered.
she could have lived,
growing older and plainer still,
laughing with her children's children.

BEING JUST PILGRIMS

Being just pilgrims
on the road;
I saw your kind face,
You shared bread
And the rhythm of walking together.
I knew I could fit into the angle of your arms,
And I crawled into the shelter of your shoulder.
You fit into my soft underbelly as no one has.
I wanted so much to believe in something human,
I now have you;
Twinkle in your eyes,
Tired feet,
And your willingness to believe in me
Being on the road,
Just pilgrims together.

BREATHING LESSONS

To keep the tears from falling
Just sit and breathe.
Do not open your mouth,
Do not begin to remember,
Just count the breaths,
In and out;
Left side, right side,
Let them stretch out on the diaphragm,
Holding down the fort.

FAITH

I want to be a path for the way miracles
Just shower down
Shot through all the fabric of molecules
Which other people think are perfectly solid;
I can see what is mostly air and magic,
Just a scrim curtain for what God is really doing
As we go about
What we think is our business.

If my own faith
Is strong enough,
It will be a flow of energy into their molecules,
Like vitamin C in the specially fortified orange juice;
Till they may notice they are getting stronger,
They will be more resistant than ever to the
Cynicism they were loaded down with,
Just the day before.

MARRIAGE, TOO, HAS SEASONS

All things that live, that are organic,
Grow and change, and die back in winter.
Oh, naivete; to think a harvest moon
Will hang upon the lowest branch forever;
And summer fruit be always within reach.
Lotus eaters always fail to notice fall;
The fading glory of the fruit upon the trees,
The last marvel; flaming cascades of leaves.

Suddenly bleak December is upon us,
And the frost, and bitter morning air,
And what seemed joyful in the spring
Is dour and gloomy in the January rain.

All choices bring within them limits;
You are not other lovers, only you,
I am not the goddess of your dreaming,
And harried, weary, I come home to you.

Divorce is commonly the remedy prescribed,
Instead of waiting for the spring;
One may as well root up the trees and bulbs
Which wait for March and April.
Why have a garden? Teach us patience,
And to hope; and to plant for months ahead,
Because in winter, love's not dead,
Just resting and developing the roots–

Another summer will bring canopies of green,
And ripe and golden fruit,
And I will smile again at you
And take your hand again, and move
With you beyond the stairs we climb;
And sing new songs of joy and tenderness.

And bursting with the fruit of patient winters,
Fill your outstretched hands with paradise.

I COULD HAVE BEEN A LADY

I move so quickly and cautiously now,
I put my armor on.

 I had to leave the room of butterflies,
The indolent ladies in pastels;
Leaning over the tea cups and silver plate,
I was called away by an urgent voice in the hall
"There is so much blood—come now!"

 I could have been a lady,
Wearing the lemon chiffon dress,
Drinking tea from china cups.

I made bandages of all the petticoats,
I made myself into an army;
All my arms and legs are paramedics.

Still, I gaze out the window
Over the heads of the wounded,
And remember the birdsong and lilacs,
I remember twirling like a girl
In the lemon chiffon dress.

IGUAZU FALLS,
Paraguay, 1973

The slab of water falling from the continental shelf
Where the 3 countries meet at the Devil's throat,
Is like a whole continent of water.

One wonders that there could possibly be enough water
To keep falling and falling,
Brown, white, caramel, lacy,
Slabs of granite, streaks of blue,
Mists rising; birds playing up and down the slopes,
And gliding on the updrafts.

We come here hot and dusty,
There is not enough clean water in the country,
All the rivers are brown,
The towns are full of mud in the rainy season,
And dust in the dry.
Here is the hotel with showers and tubs,
We luxuriate, get clean, and then walk
In the irrigated garden,
With the parrots and palm trees,
And the blue iridescent butterflies,
Fluttering amazingly around us.
Colonialism looks like a blessing here.

They will sign a treaty to build a dam:
They will owe us for at least 30 years,
More likely forever.
American tractors and ingenuity,
To build a dam (outbidding the Japanese)
To harness this continental shelf of water,
Bringing electricity to indigenous people
Who hardly need it yet;
Then will come the restless desiring,
The loss of community,
The increase of economic measurable parameters,
Asphalt, roads, cars, diesel fuel, pollution,
Factories, pesticides,
Inexorable progress
Flowing over the cliffs
At the accelerated pace
Of the biggest waterfall in the world,
Down into the Devil's throat.
Forgive me if I step back from the edge
And just watch the multiple rainbows over the top.

"I LET HER GO GENTLY"

I let her go gently,
My mother; she said:
Like a leaf down the stream,
Eight weeks flew by.
Lessons I didn't want to learn
Filled my days.

Now I am glad;
I understand so much deeper,
 I loved her till the end
In all the littlest ways.

Now I could teach someone else,
Now, I am not afraid of dying.

IN THE GRAVEYARD

There is a boy
In this graveyard,
Whose mother's arms are empty;
And her particular griefs
And loss of hope
Call to us still,
As we walk on the soft lawn
In the quiet daylight,
 To watch our children
With deeper eyesight:
Watch in the night
And in the shadows,
Holding our arms open in embrace.

PATTYCAKE

If I were a pie,
You would cut me open
And let the four and twenty blackbirds fly away
Before you started to eat me.

And they would sing and sing.

MI AMOR, MI COMPAÑERO DEL CAMINO

Oh, my love,
Sweet pilgrim companion;
Through thick and thin we have rolled
Like stones down this road,
Knowing how to arrive,
Though never first.

Whispering "freedom" like guitars in the night,
Singing with the crickets and frogs,
Hiding from the moon,
Full of revolutionary plans and dreams,
Written on whitewashed walls;
And scrounging for meals.

Elbow to elbow,
Believing in everything grand,
The murals of theological art,
The plumed serpent
Uncoiling in our blood;
Unconquered, though poor.
In full communion with saints
Who precede and follow us.

I drink to you,
The whole moon going down my throat
Like fire,
Like ice,
Take me in your arms,
Before the prison doors shut.

MOONBEAMS IN A JAR

(Would you like to swing on a star?
Carry moonbeams home in a jar;
And be better off than you are—
Or would you like to...   ) 1940's song

These Moonbeams
I bring home to you
In this jar,
I place upon the table.

You did not sing
Nor did you lie,
You brought me bread
And rosemary
With ordinary hands.

I gathered these unnecessary moonbeams
Strewn by the mystery of night;
And put them here on the table
To thank you.

I know I am better off with bread,
But I have loved moonbeams;
They glance along the glass
And curve to make it crystal,
Improbably brilliant,
Sweetly ethereal
On ordinary nights.

WRESTLING WITH THE ANGEL

Again and again,
I walk away wounded.

Again, I feel the foreboding of the oncoming night;
Knowing it will come again,
My need to struggle,
My need to win,
The angel knows it must defeat and wound me.

Silence, as the shadows lengthen,
 The dew falls softly on the garden,
And I wait again for the angel
To lock me in the terrible embrace.

Is there another way to learn?
Do I need to get this close to death?
Why without this freshened wound
Would I be paralyzed;
And only chaff, not grain?

Something which loves war
Some thick-souled animal
Lives within me;
Wanting the blood and battle,
The focused tears and anger
The knife-edged suffering.

Tonight,
Again tonight.

MRI SCAN

The sound was, I think, B flat;
It seemed I was inside a giant tuning fork.
Trombones were blowing in the alar bones
Of my hips,
Saxophones warbled up my legs,
The Bassoon was snaking up my spine
Mournful as the lamentation psalms.

I was lost in deepest fog,
But resonating with the foghorn;
All my cells were humming in B flat,
Like worker bees that know
Their hive's language.

Then I heard the whisper of
Angels, singing in an echo of heaven.

All the cells were tuned,
Like an orchestra ready to play.
God was directing,
I was all the violins,
Shimmering that B flat sound.
God said "keep playing clear and straight,
Nothing complicated."

He wanted all my cells to sing
While He Himself took over the melodic line.

MY SON

My son is growing all around me,
In me,
 Through me,
In spite of me,
Beyond me;
 On my bones and back,
In my thoughts and worries,
In the heartache,
In the nightmares,
In the pacing up and down,
Watching the moon through the windows,
Through the worn rosary beads,
Which were my father's,
Slipping through my fingers

MY MAILBOX

Send money.
Please send money.
We desperately need money.
The people are starving.
These people have no roofs over their heads.
These people have no medicines.
These people are dying of AIDS.
These poor children have no dreams;
Please give them a future.
Send money.
We are trying to help.
We are so pitifully few.
We are trying not to be angry with you for your overabundance.
We resent your plentiful larders.
We hate your white, perfumed skin;
We despise your uncalloused, lotion-soft hands.
Send money.
You are so kind.
Please be more generous next time.
In case you forget, we will write again soon.
Send money.

ON THE BENCH IN FRONT OF THE CLINIC

    1. (the young woman's voice)

He said he loved me
And I believed him.
I thought it meant forever,
Like Cinderella and her prince.
But he said
"Hey baby, I just meant
I wanna bliss ya –
No way I wanna baby,
No way I'll be tied down."
I thought we'd go to the park
On weekends,
Play with our baby in the sun;
Watch kids on swings and merry-go-rounds.
We'd save our money,
I'd work hard;
We'd buy a nice old house
In a place with lots of trees,
And eat spaghetti Thursday nights.
But he didn't really mean it,
No, he didn't mean it.
So here I am at the Clinic,
And you can take it back:
Hey, God,
Would you take my baby back
And rock it in your arms?

2. (the old lady's voice)

Oh, please, come home with me:
I have an empty cradle
And I will hold your baby when he cries;
My son is in the army
And I can hardly sleep;
(It would help if I could rock your baby
back to sleep)
I will fix some dinner:
Are you hungry?
Let me feed you,
We can sit together by the light;
No, it won't be easy,
But if we work together
All of us can make it through the night.

3. Evensong (both voices)

Together we can do it,
I know we can get through it,
Let's just start with dinner
I am hungry, and I'm thinner,
Maybe God is listening to our prayers;
I guess I'll take my chances that he cares.

PRAYER FOR THE BLUEBIRD

I was praying for happiness
At least for the bells of recollection,
And I knew
The bluebird would begin to sing,
And remind me
That singing is the purest prayer.

I sing to You,
I sing of Your creation,
Of mystery and gift,
Wisdom, beauty, breath and spirit.
I thank You,
Even for the hardest things,
Even for what I cannot understand.
I thank you for the vulnerability I was afraid of;
For dependence,
For brokenness,
For pain;
Because even with suffering,
You sent the promise
Of ecstasy beyond knowing.

Even death cannot stop
The true singing,
The real joy.

The air will fill with light,
The joy will be like light,
When light is speeding and blending with mass,
Becoming the bluebird singing.

PRAYING WITH BOTH HANDS

The baby's heartbeat slowed to a dull thud.
The meconium was thick as mud—
Thick and sticky as the mud the Israelites
Used to build bricks for making the pyramids,
When they were slaves in Egypt.

The parents' faces were tired and scared.
And so I prayed with both hands,
Slipped the forceps in, to lift the baby—
Lift the head, hugging the cheekbones,
With a mighty effort,
Like bringing the children out of Egypt,
Like Miriam,
Lifting Moses from the muddy wadi.
Praise to you, Lord God of Hosts.
The pink baby
With the glorious cry
Of clean lungs,
Singing out loud to her parents and to you—
Blessed be You,
Lord God of All Creation!

RAIN GOD

You who are the rain,
You,
 Who are the heaven it falls from,
Come down to me who lie here
Like a thirsty field in August,
With only dust and thorns and milkweed;
With these parched lips,
Too cracked and dry,
Too weak to praise You.

Yes,
 You be the rain,
That falls from heaven on this thirsty field.

RUMPELSTILTSKIN'S MAID

I have been trying to spin straw into gold
 In this dank dungeon,
The wet-hay smell of winter
Fills this closet;
And shadows are like monsters on the stone walls.

 I know I will be hung in the morning
If this impossible task isn't done.

My eyes well up,
Every molecule of air is filled with despair.
My hands are bleeding
From straw running through them,
Coarse and prickly and dry,
Over the wooden wheel.

I cannot make the straw even into thread.
Gold?
All I can think of is cornfields in summer.

My back bends over the wheel
My sore back,
My aching arms,
My empty stomach,
Dreading the dawn.

THE GEESE

Geese mate for life, and fly
Silver down breasts in rain,
White in sunlight,
Wind smoothing them to silk.

On the horizon
Maps unfolding;
Remembered
Wetlands and fields,
This lake where the babes were born;
That cluster of trees
Where we waited out a storm.

Uncle, where will we be tomorrow?
Fly with me on the shoulder
I will teach you how to know.

THE REAL RAPUNZEL

Rapunzel was locked in a tower
And the witch cackled as the threw away the key;
News spread far and wide, but slowly;
And there were no princes in the neighborhood.

Years passed.

Rapunzel grew wrinkled and wizened.
Her hair hung like grey fog from the tower window.
Rats scurried on the floor,
 Spiders were her only friends.
She grew weary of watching the horizon,
And then nearsighted.

The prince was young and handsome.
Riding on a great white horse, in shining armor.
He had heard of the beauty in the tower.
He called "Rapunzel, Rapunzel, let down your hair."
Her heart lifted and she rejoiced,
And let down her hair, in silvery glory.
But he saw her face, the old crone;
He sighed with disappointment, and turned away.

Rapunzel watched him ride away.
And cried until her tears were gone.
She lived out her days,
Whispering to spiders,
 Playing with mice.

And the prince married a merry maid,
And they lived happily ever after.

WATCHING YOU PLAY THE PIANO

If I had known,
In that golden moment so long ago,
That it was going to be a musical desert
From there to here, a Sahara;
I would not have looked away
Or lost a moment's concentration on your hands.
I would have heard the notes
With all my being,
With no distractions,
As a person dips their hands and drinks
At the oasis after days in the desert,
And nothing as exquisite as that water
Can be described.

As the throat parched beyond knowing
That water exists, are
My memories of hearing you play
The piano
That night.
And I was only half-aware,
Throwing away those moments,
Assuming the next 40 or 50 years
Would be a nightly performance,
And I could watch whenever
I felt like it.

Squandered beauty
I would hoard now in wells
With armed guards,
With strongmen,
With alarm systems;
Like a father
Who wants to bring back the daughter
Who has run away;
Run away with the fiddler,
The one bewitching person
In the whole village
Who could make an oasis in the desert.

WHITE MOTHS IN MOONLIGHT

moonlight, thick on the branches,
shadows deep as ravines.

white moths
fluttering like blossoms,
dizzyingly dancing
around my face,
weaving a lace of wings around me;
my hands among them confusing
their dance; as I try
to brush them toward the white-faced
moonflowers.
all around me redwoods breathe
into my breath,
tipping new wine into me,
 light, bright air!
the white moths, whirling,
 circle me
 like the tail of the Milky Way.

LIVE THE QUESTIONS

" You must live the questions themselves, like seeds.
Someday the answers will rise out of you like gardens"
Rilke

The girl who didn't have herpes
Has a mom who is dying of cancer.
All pain is relative;
There is peace sometimes in the worst day,
The day the bomb fell and caused your life to be a crater of moonscape.
The day you felt even breathing caused the most exquisite pain.
The girl on the phone is gasping and crying,
And saying that she just couldn't face having herpes.
As if one diagnosis made the other impossible.
Lightning is not supposed to strike twice.
The silence is profound, and you can be in it.
The words feel like cold oatmeal in your dry mouth.
"You don't have herpes.
I am so sorry about your mom".

SANDWICHES

Just in case another Columbine happens,
Or someone runs a red light,
Or you hear only terrible messages all day,
Bossy, negative and mean,
I pack these little thoughts of love
Into your sandwiches;
With the peanut butter,
Into the jam,
Sweet and thick on the tongue.

I swirl them onto bread for your lunch,
Hoping they will give you the fullness of heart,
The joy of the wide blue sky,
The patience and fortitude,
Sunshine and fresh air in your soul,
To make it to the end of the day;
Till I can see your face again
Till I know you are safe,
You precious darling of my heart.

These are my tools,
Peanut butter and jam;
To build a shelter against suffering and pain.

You precious darling of my heart,
Carrying this brown paper bag of sandwiches.

THE HOSE WITH THE KINK

The hose with the kink
Is getting older and stiffer,
And it has gotten a sort of frost of old rubber on it.
I drag it around the flowerbeds;
Going back to unkink it,
So the water will flow through.

I have used this hose
For years as a metaphor for strokes;
Almost daily
I tell a patient whose blood pressure is high
That in the body,
When you add the fine-spray nozzle,
That exact happenstance occurs;
Pressure builds up in a place that got kinked,
 It cracks and spills,
Like an aneurysm of a damaged blood vessel;
And if it is in the brain, the flooded part
Becomes a stroke.
Something becomes crippled;
You might lose the ability to think or talk or walk.
I scare people into taking their medicine.
They thank me for the vivid lesson.

In the patio,
The hose with the kink
Has a fine spray jetting up from it,
And I see the rainbow it makes
With prisms of sunlight in the water.
Suddenly, I the aging gardener wonder
 About the blessing and the curse.

THE GUARDIAN ANGEL OF THE RED BUS
(Paraguay, 1974)

The guardian angel of the red bus
Watches over lambs and sheep and flapping tarps,
Pigs and stoats and chickens,
Bicycles and bundles lashed on at angles,
And people, spilling out the doors.

Inside, the seated peasants gaze out the windows
Or straight ahead;
Glad to be out of the sun,
Glad to be sitting; stoically patient for the ride.

Oh, guardian angel, keep us safe!

On the terrible pock-marked, rutted roads,
On the hairpin turns;
On the muddy banks where the river curves
Too close to the road;
On the places where the cows have to cross
Before and behind us;
On the narrow gorges where the deer
Might leap in front of us,
Confused by our passage.

This red bus, with the solid sides
Has holes in the floor and a temperamental motor;
Please help us make it;
On these balding tires,
And with only this much diesel,
Before the hard rains come and close the road
With ruts that look like river banks;
Before the hens get too shocked and jostled to lay eggs,
Before the pigs catch cold, in the burlap sacks,
Grunting and whining overhead;
Before we roar into the capitol
In this black cloud of diesel exhaust and gritty faces,
And numbly unbend our paralyzed legs and arms,
To walk away from this most holy vehicle;

You, dear angel, please watch over this red bus
 Till we can go back home.

ÉLAN VITAL

You cock your head like a parrot,
You raise your eyebrows,
While spreading your fingers
As you wave upward; hands open;
You almost smile.

You appreciate the ambiguity,
You have nothing to add.

We have heard it all before,
All the words and reasons,
We have fought all these fights,
We have compromised,
We have backed down.

Now we just hold hands and smile.

Or, if you are across the room,
You nod and shrug;
And we understand how much affection
There is in that.

DANCING WITH THE MINISTER OF THE INTERIOR
Paraguay 1973

The look of the man was possibly
Like the captain of the secret police;
Mafioso,
Grandfatherly,
With a self-satisfied beer belly.

He arrived with his mistress,
A long-boned, white-skinned woman
With lovely grey eyes,
And a cloud of dark hair.
She would have made a good model
For a life-drawing class.

Being one of the local dignitaries,
The Peace Corps Volunteer,
I was asked to dance.
He was a good dancer,
Light on his feet,
Like me.

We danced the Paraguayan polka
In a clearing in the woods
By Minas Cue;
The fat PCV young woman,
And the fat minister.

How would I know
What his theory of justice was,
Or his desire to protect the interior,
The heartland of the country?

ALBONDIGA SOUP

"Nana, I have a fever."

"I will make soup.
I will make albondiga soup
With the secret ingredient."

It cooks on the stove,
And the whole house fills
With the smell of healing;
Moist steam
Fragrant with herbs—
The albondigas
Go into the hot steaming soup;
The flour-covered meatballs,
Held together with breadcrumbs and egg;
A hint of mint,
The secret ingredient,
And always a few finely chopped onions.

"Here, mi Corazón,
This will make you stronger."

CANNING TOMATOES

In August,
We picked tomatoes, in the heat;
Gleaning the fields like Ruth and Naomi,
Behind our mother.
 Bending and twisting, hands out; in the sticky-leaved vines;
Hot, sweaty, smeared with rotten tomato drippings and
blackened hands.

Crates of warm, ripe tomatoes
Filled the kitchen with that dusty tomato scent.
We washed the quart bottles
Saved from last year's batch;
And new lids and rings,
Boiling them in the turkey pan on the stove,
Rattling, with steamy lids, all afternoon.

Mom rosy-cheeked, and all of us sweating,
Peeling the tomatoes,
Quartering them,
Cooking them,
Then pouring them carefully into the
Wide-mouthed, hot crystal jars.

By the time dad came home,
6 dozen or more quarts of tomatoes,
Red-red; in shiny, full bottles,
To last all winter,
Filled all the surfaces in the kitchen.
Almost everything mom knew how to cook needed those
tomatoes.

 They tasted better than any commercial ones;
All the fields of California, and the sunshine,
Caught in quart bottles, that bright red-ripe color.

ISABEL

White-haired, blue-eyed, and stately,
In beautiful clothes,
In the purple silk Spanish shawl,
Embroidered with white flowers,
She turns on the stair,
Looking down,
Looking back.

Regal,
They all said.
Gracious,
Lady-like;
But did she pirouette?
I ask,
Did she pirouette before the gilded mirrors?
Did she adjust the mantilla with the rose in her hair,
With the light on the glittering alexandrite ring on her hand;
Did she dance a little to see the fringe of the shawl
Shimmer in its silky white way?
My grandmother danced—
Was she like her mother?
Did my great-grandmother dance?
Or was she always measured and stately,
Moving through the room like a ship at sea,
With a gracious tilt to her head, and a half-smile?
She had a sense of humor they said.
But was it really funny, like my Nana's—
Who could make you laugh till the tears rolled
Down your cheeks,
And glad the whole time!
I would like to know.
When she turned to go up the stairs,
In the shimmering silk purple shawl,
With the white flowers, elegant and lovely,
Did you sigh because the life was leaving the room?

Did you feel when she walked in, the weight of vanity,
Or did you simply become bedazzled,
When she shone like sunshine on you?

She was gone before I came,
And I cannot get the feel of how she wore that purple silk shawl.
I know she drove the spring wagon,
Full of camping gear to Matilija in the summer.
I know she was a great shopper,
And she loved to go to parties in Los Angeles.
Was she loved at the parties?
Was she moody or withdrawn at home?
Did she have headaches?
Did she love music?
Did she worry about her son's drinking,
Her daughters' boyfriends,
Mourn excessively over the two daughters who died?
All I can see is how she turned
To go up the stairs,
The purple shawl around her shoulders,
And the field of white flowers scattered down her back.

PICNIC AT THE CHUMASH BURIAL GROUND, 1963

When the UCLA archeologists
Told us that this was an area sacred to the natives,
We understood why we always could find the little
Shells pierced for necklaces, and arrowheads here.
The gently mounded hill above,
The little creek below,
Made it a perfect place for a picnic.

We had a big basket of food;
Sandwiches, thermoses of milk and juice,
Cookies.
Wading in the creek,
Looking for arrowheads,
Singing songs.

Were the ancestors looking kindly on us,
Or did they see us as invaders,
Desecrating their land?
We were careful not to disturb things,
We picked up all our trash.
Was it wrong to take their arrowheads?
They would not need them now…
I had a little necklace of the beads.
The Chumash walked all the way to the beach
In Ventura or even Carpinteria to get the shells.
Did they have picnics on the beach?
Did they stay many days before they came home?
Did they eat sandwiches?
Mom said they ate acorns.
Acorns are very bitter.
Later, at a museum in Yosemite,
I learned how they got the bitterness out—
A laborious process that took days.
They wore little clothes, as it was a mild climate.

There weren't many relics from their time here.
What did they do when it rained?
Was the burial ceremony elaborate?
Did they sing songs?
Did they have drums and stringed instruments?
Now I wish I remembered.
I just remember leaning over the little creek,
Looking for pollywogs.
Willow branches leaned from the other side.
A dragonfly flew by me, the first I ever saw.

PLAY THE SAXOPHONE FOR ME, JAMIE

Sweet blue-eyed boy,
Play your horn;
Play the bubbles from that golden throat;
Make a little champagne for me,
Here and now.

And if you play the blues,
Let it be blue-skies blues;
A tolerable pain,
With some champagne in the remedy.
Let it be over the rainbow
Hope for the future;
Blue-bird of happiness on your shoulder,
And sunny days coming on.

Pour me a funny valentine,
I'll smile with my heart;
Bubbling up from your fingers and throat,
Let me hear the lazy river of summer evenings
 The big fat moon rising low on the hills,
The moan of the train in the distance
When my honey's finally comin' home.

Keep the good times in your soul;
Like the best melodies,
Written indelibly in your memory,
Ready to come bubbling out
When we need a little magic,
Need a little stardust;
Honey, blow your horn;
Pour out a big golden valentine of song.

THIS JAR OF JAM

I made this jam
From the fruit of today,
Your conversation,
Ripe as berries:
Olallieberries, tart and sweet and summer-warm
Your laughter,
Like cups of sugar,
Gently mounded,
And the way the sunshine hit the kitchen window
At a Vermeer angle in August.

By the time I put the lid down
On the steamy wide-mouth jar
I knew we would get a gold medal at the fair.

The moist steam heating my cheeks like peaches,
I laugh at your amusing banter,
My berry-stained hands rubbing down the apron
Over my housewifely plumpness,
Which I see brings the twinkle to your appraising eye.
The ruby-warm jam is filling the quilted jar,
And I am satisfied with its perfection.

HOLY GROUND

And if I walk here barefoot,
And kneel,
And rub the earth into my knees,
Will it bless me?
Will the angel bend above me and touch my shoulders,
Will the hand of the Lord be upon me;
Will I hear His voice?

I have not hardened my heart.
I have come here on my knees.
I have taken off my shoes.

I feel the sun on my back.
I hear the song of the birds.
The air here is gentle.

Psalms come to my mouth,
To praise You,
To praise You.

Order Form

To order additional copies, fill out this form and send it along with your check or money order to:

Martina Nicholson
PO Box 890
Soquel CA   95073-0890
Cost per copy $8.00 includes P&H.

Ship _____ copies of *My Throat Is Full of Songbirds* to:

Name_____

Address:_____

City/State/Zip:_____

___ Check for signed copy

Please tell us how you found out about this book.
___ Friend   ___ Internet
___ Book Store   ___ Radio
___ Newspaper   ___ Magazine
___ Other _____